THE
SINKING
of
THE *TITANIC*

A HISTORY PERSPECTIVES BOOK

Marcia Amidon Lusted

Published in the United States of America by Sleeping Bear Press
Ann Arbor, Michigan
www.sleepingbearpress.com

Consultants: George Behe, author, *On Board RMS Titanic: Memories
of the Maiden Voyage*; Marla Conn, ReadAbility, Inc.
Editorial direction: Red Line Editorial

ISBN 978-1-58536-901-0

Printed in the United States of America
Corporate Graphics Inc.

10 9 8 7 6 5 4 3 2 1

TABLE OF CONTENTS

In this book, you will read about the *Titanic*'s sinking from three perspectives. Each perspective is based on real things that happened to real people who were aboard the ship. As you'll see, the same event can look different depending on one's point of view.

1

William Davies
Crew Member

It was April 14, 1912, and one of the coldest nights of the year I could remember. I crouched in the crow's nest 50 feet above the deck of the *Titanic*. I was very excited to be hired for the crew of this brand-new luxury ship. I had read about it in the newspapers. The *Titanic* was said to be unsinkable. The ship had 16 **compartments** inside her **hull**. Each compartment

▲ *The* Titanic *was designed to be unsinkable.*

was designed with watertight doors that would close

automatically if there was a leak. This would contain

the seawater in the compartment and prevent the

THINK ABOUT IT

▶ Determine the main point of the first paragraph and pick out one piece of evidence that supports it.

entire hull of the ship from filling with water.

My job was to act as a lookout. I spent my time scanning the sea in front of the ship, looking for anything that might get in the way. Tonight the crew was worried about icebergs. We were moving through the cold waters of the North Atlantic Ocean. Captain Edward Smith had received warnings about possible ice, but he did not want to slow the ship's speed. He was hoping to show how fast his new ship could travel. Now the clock was creeping toward midnight. It was only a little above freezing, and my teeth were chattering. Stuart, the other lookout, was blowing on his hands to keep them warm.

I watched the darkness in front of the ship. I saw a slight haze that made me blink my eyes to

clear them. Then suddenly a huge shape loomed
out of the inky night. It was an iceberg, and only
500 yards away! I quickly reached over and rang the
warning bell three times. Then I picked up the
telephone that connected to the bridge, where the

▲ *In 1912, the* Titanic *was the largest ship in the world.*

ship was steered. "Iceberg right ahead," I said urgently.

Moments after I saw the iceberg, I felt a vibration. The ship scraped the iceberg on her **starboard** side. I saw chunks of ice fall on the starboard deck. They shattered and skittered on the polished wood. The iceberg was huge. It looked to be 100 feet high. And we'd been told most of an iceberg is often underwater, where it can't be seen. It was likely this iceberg was even bigger than we thought.

A few moments after hitting the iceberg, I felt the engines stop. I looked at Stuart. Alarm showed on his face, as I'm sure it did in mine. When I climbed down from the crow's nest, other crew members told me that water was pouring into six of

SECOND SOURCE

▶ Find another source that describes the moment when the iceberg was first seen. Compare the information there to the information in this source.

the ship's watertight compartments. The iceberg had ripped a hole in *Titanic*'s side. The first officer had ordered the watertight doors of those six compartments to be closed, but it was too late.

SOS

The *Titanic* struck the iceberg at 11:40 p.m. on April 14. At 12:15 a.m. on April 15, Captain Smith ordered one of the ship's officers to calculate the exact position of the ship. Then he had the ship's radio operator tap out the first **distress signal** in Morse code. By the time the ship sank, 70 messages were sent back and forth between the *Titanic* and other ships in the area. Ships of several nationalities started to come to the aid of the *Titanic*. But the ship that was closest to the *Titanic*, the *Californian*, did not receive the distress messages. Its radio operator was asleep.

crow's nest

▲ *The iceberg was spotted from the crow's nest, near the front of the ship.*

Six flooded compartments were more than the ship's designers ever planned for. The *Titanic* would not be able to float with so many compartments flooded. The ship was filling with water. How could this be happening to the unsinkable ship?

▲ *This modern-day image shows how large an iceberg can be. Still, no one imagined the* Titanic *would hit one and fill with water.*

2

Lucy Winn-Norton
First-Class Passenger

▲ *Margaret Tobin Brown*

We had been hearing for months that the *Titanic* was the ultimate in luxury. When my husband, Lord Peter Norton, told me he had booked us first-class tickets on the *Titanic*'s maiden voyage, I could not have been more excited. What better way to return home from our European tour than on board the most luxurious ship ever built?

We took a train to southern England and arrived at the Southampton docks. The *Titanic* towered above us. Her white sides gleamed above the black hull, and her four graceful cream and black funnels reached toward the sky. As we moved up the **gangway** into the

WHO'S WHO

The *Titanic* was the most fashionable way for wealthy people to travel by ship. Because of that, many famous passengers were aboard. Isidor Straus, who started the Macy's department store, died with his wife, Rosalie Ida. Benjamin Guggenheim was another wealthy man on board. As the ship sank, he is remembered as saying, "We've dressed in our best and are prepared to go down like gentlemen." Probably the most famous *Titanic* survivor was Margaret Tobin Brown. She was a wealthy and brave woman who tried to get Lifeboat No. 6 to return to the site of the sinking to find survivors. She was given the nickname "the unsinkable Molly Brown."

ship, we were greeted by our own personal **steward**. He took us to our stateroom near the center of the ship. It was grander than many of the grandest European hotels! We had a sitting room, bedroom, dressing room, and private bath. I had many trunks to store all the clothing I brought, and there was room for them all.

We even had our own **promenade deck**. What a wonderful convenience! I was delighted to be able to stroll along it in the fresh sea air in privacy. There are times when one just doesn't want to have to be part of the social groups on the public decks. Peter was pleased to see there was even a telephone. This could be used for calls only to other passengers, but it was a convenience that was rarely seen on a ship. We had traveled on luxury ships before, but *Titanic* was

SECOND SOURCE

▶ Find another source that describes what it was like to be a first-class passenger. Compare that information to this source.

▲ *A replica of the grand staircase shows the* Titanic's *luxury.*

▲ *A re-creation of a first-class dinner shows the fine dining first-class passengers enjoyed.*

by far the most elegant and modern ship I had ever been on. It seemed to have every comfort and convenience we could think of.

We spent our first days pleasantly enough. We walked along the promenade deck and had tea at the café on A Deck. I visited with other passengers, read, and wrote letters. We even attended concerts by the ship's orchestra.

On the night of April 14, I retired to my room to read before going to sleep. Close to midnight, I felt an odd vibration. Then my attendant, Tess, was at my side, telling me our steward had told us to put on our **lifebelts**. She said the ship's engines had stopped and we were in trouble. I did not see the need to put on my lifebelt, as the ship was said to be unsinkable.

▲ *Mostly women and children were given seats in the lifeboats.*

The lifebelts were bulky and my bed was so warm. But Tess insisted, and soon Peter was there as well, still in his evening clothes. He told me the ship had struck an iceberg. Though neither of us believed there was any danger, the crew had orders to get us all up on deck and into lifeboats.

Tess helped me into my warmest fur coat and my lifebelt. Together with Peter and his valet, Charles, we climbed up to the deck. The night air was bitingly cold. Around us there was confusion as lifeboats were lowered into the water. Distress rockets lit up the sky like fireworks. Peter quickly moved us to the front of the line for lifeboats, past the passengers from the other classes. The steward was going to allow Peter into the lifeboat, even though it should have been women and children only. Peter

ANALYZE THIS

▶ Analyze two narratives in this book that describe the moment when passengers were getting into lifeboats. How are they different?

▲ *Passengers were rescued by the ship* Carpathia.

refused to get on. Instead, he helped me and Tess into
a lifeboat filled with other women and children. Some
of them were from **steerage**, and one child was nearly
blue with cold. I almost did not realize that Peter was
not with us. As the boat slowly reached the surface of
the ocean, he called down to us saying a farewell. It
was the last time I ever saw my dear husband.

3

Maggie Donavan
Steerage Passenger

I was curled up in my bunk in the steerage class of *Titanic*, trying to get warm. Mum was snoring in her bunk, and the little ones were whimpering in their sleep. Suddenly I felt the whole ship shudder. Steerage is located near the bottom of the ship, four decks below the ship's main deck (called the boat deck, because lifeboats were kept there).

The vibration surprised me and felt like it was right by me. Our cabin was in the back of the ship. We did have a tiny porthole window, but I couldn't see what was going on.

I asked Mum if she'd felt it. She hushed me, so I wouldn't wake my younger brothers, and said she had. Soon I heard voices shouting and felt the ship's rumbling engines stop. Down here in steerage, we had gotten used to hearing those huge engines day and night. The movement of the ship was stronger too, and my insides often rolled so much that I couldn't eat. We had barely any space to go out on the rear deck that was just for steerage passengers, and we always had to watch out for rats.

This set us apart from the fancier people traveling above us in the first- and second-class cabins. Someone told me they paid as much as $4,000 for the tickets to stay in the fancy four-room parlor suites. I couldn't even imagine that much money. It took Pa years to

▲ *A replica of a steerage cabin shows how small the living space was.*

save up for the $20 for each of our steerage tickets. Once I squeezed my way onto the steerage deck. From where I stood I could see the ladies in their silks, lace, and fancy hats. They were walking on the deck reserved just for first-class passengers. It was higher and farther away from our deck. We weren't allowed up there. They say, though, that steerage on the *Titanic* was

THE COST OF A TICKET

How much did it cost to travel on the *Titanic*? Only the very rich could afford first-class cabins. A ticket for a cabin cost $150 (about $3,500 today). For a first-class parlor suite with three or four rooms, the price was more than $4,000 (about $100,000 today). A ticket in steerage cost between $15 and $40 (about $350 to $930 today).

much better than on other ships. We actually had our own cabins instead of sharing one big room. And we had running water and electricity. They even gave us our meals. We thought ourselves lucky.

I climbed down from my bunk and threw my shawl over my nightgown. I crept out into the hallway and made my way down to the dining **saloon** where the steerage passengers ate their meals. Many other people had gathered there. One of the steerage passengers who had spoken to a crewman told us the *Titanic* had struck an iceberg. He said we should put on our lifebelts and go up to the lifeboats on the upper deck.

I quickly ran back to tell Mum, and together we got the three little ones out of bed and into the warmest clothes we could

ANALYZE THIS

▶ Analyze two accounts in this book that describe the moment when passengers first learned the ship was in trouble and they needed to leave their rooms. How are they different?

find. Mum was moaning all the while about Pa, wishing he were here instead of waiting for us in America. I concentrated on getting the lifebelts on my little brothers. Then Mum and I grabbed their hands and stumbled out to the stairways that led to the upper decks. Being steerage passengers, we had

▲ *Those in lifeboats rowed to reach the* Carpathia, *the ship that rescued survivors.*

not been allowed to use those stairs or leave our area before this. I quickly became confused by all the passageways and stairs. Other steerage passengers who did not speak English were even more lost and confused. We started to panic because we were told about rising water in another part of the ship. Finally someone pointed the way up onto the deck.

Men were loading people into the lifeboats, calling for women and children only. I was worried that perhaps only the first-class passengers would be allowed to get into the boats, and there did seem to be more of them on the deck. Luckily one of the ship's officers saw us and helped us climb into one of the big lifeboats. My brothers cried in fear when the boat creaked and swayed as it was lowered by ropes toward the dark sea.

Scared, we huddled together in the lifeboat. Steerage, second, or first class, it didn't matter. Some of the first-class ladies stayed apart at first, but soon

▲ *Newspapers around the world reported the sinking of the* Titanic *on the front page.*

we all drew together for warmth. I saw the stern of the great ship rise into the air, and then the vessel seemed to break almost in half before slowly sliding below the surface. I could hear the cries of those still on board, which made me shiver even more than the biting cold. After many terrible, cold hours, the ship *Carpathia* rescued us from our bobbing in the sea.

We were the lucky ones. After we finally reached America and found Pa, he told us more than 1,500 people died, and more steerage passengers died than passengers in any other class. Only one-fourth of steerage passengers survived. It was just too far from our quarters to the deck. Mum, the little ones, and I were very fortunate to have made it. I also found out later that the ship did not have enough lifeboats for all the passengers. Perhaps people thought they weren't

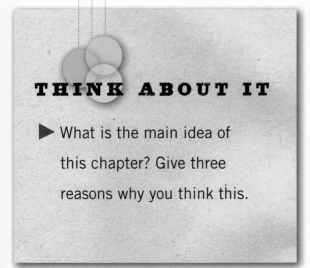

THINK ABOUT IT

▶ What is the main idea of this chapter? Give three reasons why you think this.

needed since the ship was said to be unsinkable. All I know is that I still shudder when I think about my steerage friends trapped in the cold, dark waters as *Titanic* sank.

▲ *Researchers discovered the* Titanic *at the bottom of the Atlantic Ocean in 1985.*

LOOK, LOOK AGAIN

The *Titanic* first sailed in the ocean during sea trials. This is when the new ship would have been tested to make sure the engines and steering worked properly. Look at the photograph and answer the following questions:

1. What would a crew member of the *Titanic* have thought when he saw the new ship moving through the water for the first time?

2. What might a first-class passenger think when he or she saw the ship for the first time? What might have impressed him or her the most?

3. Steerage passengers probably thought about the *Titanic* in a different way from the upper-class passengers. What might a steerage passenger be thinking and feeling when she or he saw the ship?

GLOSSARY

compartment (kuhm-PAHRT-muhnt) a separate part of a container, where things can be kept away from others

distress signal (di-STRES SIG-nuhl) a universal signal sent out by a ship or plane to say that help is needed

gangway (GANG-way) a platform for boarding a ship

hull (HUHL) the frame or body of a ship

lifebelt (LIFE-belt) a life preserver in the shape of a belt

promenade deck (prah-muh-NAHD DEK) an upper deck on a passenger ship used to enjoy the open air

saloon (suh-LOON) the dining room on a ship

starboard (STAHR-burd) the right side of a ship when facing forward

steerage (STEER-ij) the part of a ship where the cheapest cabins are located

steward (STOO-urd) a man who serves passengers on a ship

LEARN MORE

Further Reading

Chrisp, Peter. *Explore Titanic: Breathtaking New Pictures, Recreated with Digital Technology.* Hauppauge, NY: Barron's Educational Series, 2011.

Hopkinson, Deborah. *Titanic: Voices from the Disaster.* New York: Scholastic, 2012.

Stewart, Melissa. *Titanic.* Washington, DC: National Geographic, 2012.

Tarshis, Lauren. *I Survived the Sinking of the Titanic, 1912.* New York: Scholastic, 2010.

Web Sites

Titanic
http://www.history.com/interactives/titanic-interactive
Readers will find information, games, videos, and interactive features about the *Titanic* on this Web site.

Titanic: 100 Years
http://channel.nationalgeographic.com/channel/titanic-100-years
This Web site has information about the *Titanic* with links to videos, including the discovery of the wreck.

INDEX

ABOUT THE AUTHOR

Marcia Amidon Lusted is the author of 75 books and 350 magazine articles for young readers. She has been interested in the *Titanic* since she was young. She has visited the cemetery in Nova Scotia, Canada, where many of the *Titanic* victims are buried.

COMMON CORE ACTIVITIES

You need to learn about lots of things, but you also need to learn how to learn. This book encourages you to read and think critically about its content.

To guide your reading, this book includes notes that will help build the understanding and skills required by the Common Core State Standards. Look for the following callouts throughout the book:

▶ **Think about It:** The activities in this section ask you to interact with the book's content in ways required by the Common Core State Standards. You might be asked to identify a main idea, discuss surprising facts, or examine facts and ideas.

▶ **Analyze This:** These sidebars ask you to compare or contrast two or more of the narratives in the book to discover how they are similar or different.

▶ **Second Source:** These sections prompt you to find another source on this topic and compare the information there to the information in this source.